First Facts™

Community Helpers at Work

A Day in the Life of a
Doctor

by Heather Adamson

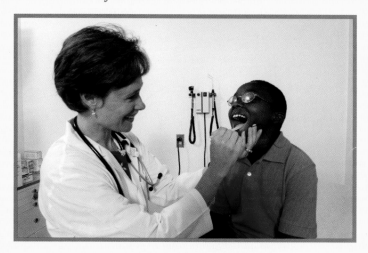

Consultant:
Bryan P. Bergeron, M.D.
Research Affiliate and Assistant Professor
Harvard Medical School and MIT
Brookline, Massachusetts

Capstone press

Mankato, Minnesota

First Facts is published by Capstone Press
151 Good Counsel Drive, P.O. Box 669, Mankato, Minnesota 56002
http://www.capstonepress.com

Library of Congress Cataloging-in-Publication Data
Adamson, Heather, 1974–
    A day in the life of a doctor/by Heather Adamson.
    p. cm.—(First facts. Community helpers at work)
    Includes bibliographical references and index.
    Contents: How do doctors begin their days?—What are rounds?—How do doctors help people?—Why do healthy people go to the doctor?—Who helps doctors?—How do doctors learn patient care?—What happens if there is an emergency?—What happens at the end of a doctor's day?
    ISBN 0-7368-2506-1 (hardcover)
    1. Medicine—Vocational guidance—Juvenile literature. 2. Physicians—Juvenile literature. [1. Physicians. 2. Occupations.] I.Title. II. Series.
R690.A236 2004
610.69'52—dc21
                 2003011451

Credits
Jennifer Bergstrom, series designer; Enoch Peterson, book designer; Gary Sundermeyer, photographer; Eric Kudalis, product planning editor

Photo Credits
All photos by Capstone Press except p. 20, Corbis

Artistic effects
Comstock; Photodisc/Siede Preis

Capstone Press wishes to thank Catherine A. Davis, M.D., for her assistance in the photographing of this book.

1 2 3 4 5 6 09 08 07 06 05 04

Table of Contents

How do doctors begin their days?

Some doctors work **shifts** in hospitals. Some doctors also work in clinics. Dr. Davis starts her day at the hospital. She wears a white coat and a **stethoscope** around her neck. She will visit patients at the hospital. Later, she will go to work at the clinic.

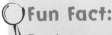

Fun Fact:
Doctors sometimes work 80 hours a week or more.

What are rounds?

Doctors make rounds to check on their patients who are in the hospital. Dr. Davis checks on a woman who had a baby.

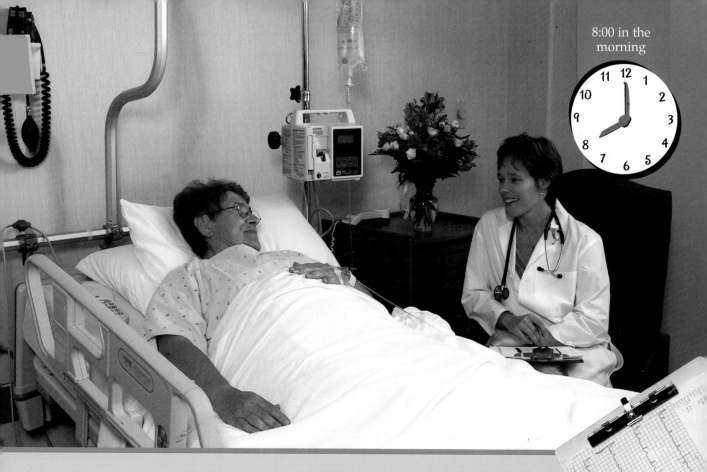

Dr. Davis also visits a patient who had **surgery** yesterday. She reads charts to see how the patient is doing. She writes orders for the nurses to follow.

How do doctors help people?

Doctors examine patients to make a **diagnosis**. Dr. Davis uses a scope to look in a patient's ear. She finds out why he is not feeling well. Dr. Davis writes a **prescription** for medicine to fight an **infection** and stop pain.

 Fun Fact:

Doctors in the United States write at least 1.5 billion prescriptions for medicine each year.

9:30 in the
morning

10:30 in the
morning

Why do healthy people go to the doctor?

Healthy people need checkups to help them stay well. Dr. Davis looks in the patient's throat. She listens to her heart and lungs. She checks **reflexes** with a soft hammer. The patient will get a shot to prevent disease and keep her healthy.

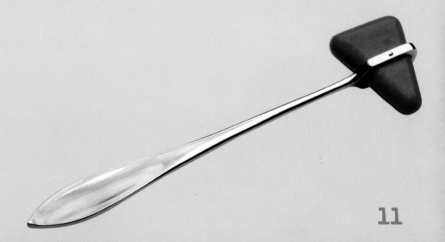

Who helps doctors?

Many people help doctors. Nurses work with patients. Office workers make appointments and keep track of charts.

Pharmacists also help doctors. They fill
doctors' prescriptions. They get medicine
ready for patients. Pharmacists explain
what the medicine is for and how to take it.

1:00 in the afternoon

Fun Fact:
Most doctors attend eight years of school after high school. They then complete three years of training.

How do doctors learn patient care?

Doctors go to school for many years to learn how to help patients. Doctors must keep learning. Dr. Davis goes to a meeting after lunch. She learns about new kinds of medicine.

What happens if there is an emergency?

Doctors work quickly in emergencies.
Dr. Davis looks at an X-ray for one patient.

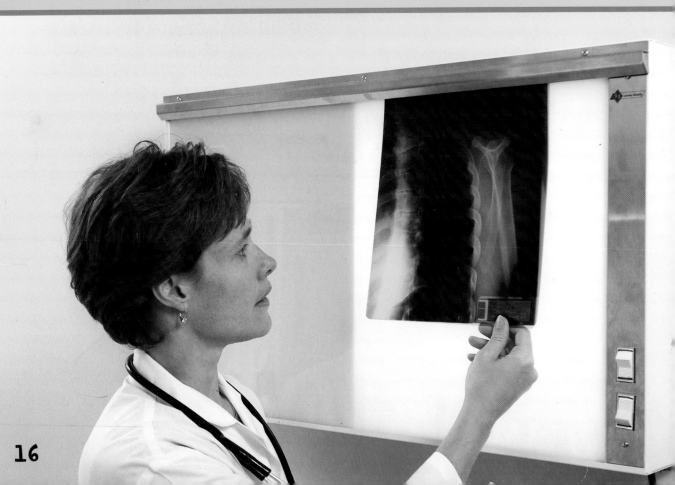

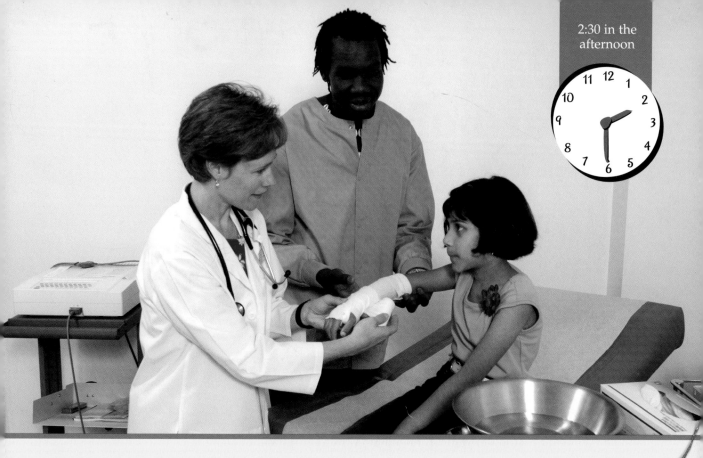

Dr. Davis helps another patient who has a broken bone. She uses a cast to hold the bone in place. Some doctors also help with emergencies at night and on weekends.

17

What happens at the end of a doctor's day?

Doctors read over reports at the end of the day. Dr. Davis explains each patient's visit into a voice recorder. Her information will be added to the patient's chart. Dr. Davis helps many people every day.

5:00 in the evening

19

Amazing But True!

In 1928, Dr. Alexander Fleming went to clean a pile of dirty lab dishes. Mold was growing in some of the dishes. The mold was killing other germs growing in the dishes. Fleming's messy lab helped him discover penicillin. This medicine is still used today.

Stethoscope

Printer

Equipment

A doctor uses rubber gloves, a scissors, and other equipment during a checkup.

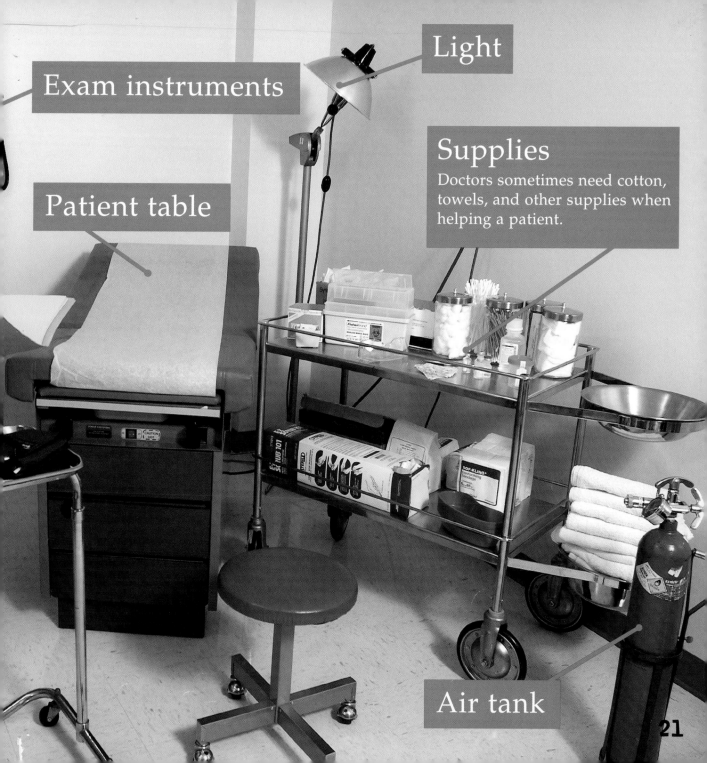

Exam instruments

Light

Supplies
Doctors sometimes need cotton, towels, and other supplies when helping a patient.

Patient table

Air tank

21

Glossary

diagnosis (dye-uhg-NOHSS-is)—the act of finding a cause for a problem or illness

infection (in-FEK-shuhn)—an illness caused by germs growing in the body

order (OR-dur)—a written request by a doctor for patient care or treatment

prescription (pri-SKRIP-shuhn)—an order for medicine from a doctor

reflex (REE-fleks)—an action that happens without a person's control or effort

shift (SHIFT)—a set amount of time to work

stethoscope (STETH-uh-skope)—a tool medical workers use to listen to a patient's heart and lungs

surgery (SUR-jer-ee)—a medical treatment that repairs or removes body parts that are sick or hurt

Read More

Christy, Lee. *I Go to Work as a Doctor.* I Go to Work As. Minneapolis: Lake Street Publishers, 2003.

Owen, Ann. *Keeping You Healthy: A Book about Doctors.* Community Workers. Minneapolis: Picture Window Books, 2004.

Internet Sites

FactHound offers a safe, fun way to find Internet sites related to this book. All of the sites on FactHound have been researched by our staff.

Here's how:
1. Visit *www.facthound.com*
2. Type in this special code **0736825061** for age-appropriate sites. Or enter a search word related to this book for a more general search.
3. Click on Fetch It button.

FactHound will fetch the best sites for you!

Index